chicken

simple and delicious easy-to-make recipes

Jean May

Marks and Spencer p.l.c.
Baker Street, London, W1U 8EP

www.marksandspencer.com

Titles in this series are subject to availability.

ISBN: 1-84273-843-7

Printed in China

Produced by the Bridgewater Book Company Ltd.

Photographer Calvey Taylor-Haw

Home Economist Ruth Pollock

The crockery featured on the following pages can be
purchased at Marks and Spencer's stores:

page 11 – plate, T/34/02148/4923 108
       – bowl, T/34/02148/4925 108

page 15 – plate, T/34/02733/1005
       – bowl, T/34/02733/1002

page 33 – plate, T34/02148/5302

NOTES FOR THE READER

- This book uses both metric and imperial measurements. Follow the same units of measurement throughout; do not mix metric and imperial.

- All spoon measurements are level: teaspoons are assumed to be 5 ml, and tablespoons are assumed to be 15 ml.

- Unless otherwise stated, milk is assumed to be full fat, eggs and individual vegetables such as potatoes are medium, and pepper is freshly ground black pepper.

- Recipes using raw or very lightly cooked eggs should be avoided by infants, the elderly, pregnant women, convalescents, and anyone suffering from an illness.

- The times given are an approximate guide only. Preparation times differ according to the techniques used by different people and the cooking times may also vary from those given. Optional ingredients, variations or serving suggestions have not been included in the calculations.

contents

introduction

Chicken is wonderfully versatile and its popularity never seems to wane. From succulent starters and snacks to full traditional roasts, this delicately flavoured bird can provide a host of tantalising dishes for every occasion. Whether that occasion is a simple lunch or an extravagant dinner party, a buffet, barbecue, picnic or supper, the practical yet delicious versatility of chicken will always come into its own.

For the health-conscious among you, chicken is amazingly low in fat, especially when cooked without the skin. It is also extremely nutritious. Chicken is rich in protein and B vitamins, especially vitamin B3, which promotes healthy skin and digestion, boosts energy and helps to lower cholesterol. Chicken is also an excellent source of magnesium, which helps to counter stress, fight depression and protect against heart attacks.

On the flavour front, chicken combines well with so many delicious foods that the possible combinations are endless. It is also inexpensive, and a little can go a long way. So what better way to capitalise on the wonderful benefits of chicken than by sampling the recipes in this book? Whatever the occasion, there is bound to be something in the following pages to suit every taste and every budget.

guide to recipe key		
	very easy	Recipes are graded as follows: 1 pea = easy; 2 peas = very easy; 3 peas = extremely easy.
	serves 4	Recipes generally serve four people. Simply halve the ingredients to serve two, taking care not to mix metric and imperial measurements.
	10 minutes	Preparation time. Where marinating or soaking are involved, these times have been added on separately: eg, 15 minutes + 30 minutes to marinate.
	10 minutes	Cooking time. Cooking times do not include the cooking of side dishes or accompaniments served with the main dishes.

chicken & prawn laksa
page 14

chicken with creamy spaghetti
page 42

chicken & barley stew
page 70

chicken pinwheels with
blue cheese & herbs, page 92

soups
& starters

Making soup at home is quick, easy
and satisfying, and an economical way of
using leftover chicken. The soups in this
section reflect the delightful flavours
of international cuisine, such as the
Thai Chicken Soup, which evokes the
unforgettable flavours of Thailand, and
the delicious Scottish Cock-a-Leekie, a
comforting soup for cold days and nights.
This section also features some very tempting
starters, such as succulent Breadcrumbed
Chicken Morsels, and sumptuous Chicken
Livers in Red Wine & Thyme.

thai chicken soup

		ingredients	
very easy	1 tbsp sesame oil or chilli oil	850 ml/1½ pints chicken stock
	2 garlic cloves, chopped	2 tbsp rice wine
serves 4	2 spring onions, trimmed and sliced	1 tbsp chopped lemon grass
	1 leek, trimmed and finely sliced	6 kaffir lime leaves, finely shredded
	1 tbsp grated fresh root ginger	200 g/7 oz fine egg noodles
15–20 minutes	1 red chilli, deseeded and finely chopped	salt and pepper
	350 g/12 oz skinless chicken breasts, cut into strips	
30 minutes		

Heat the oil in a wok or large saucepan. Add the garlic and cook over a medium heat, stirring, for 1 minute, then add the spring onions, leek, ginger and chilli and cook, stirring, for a further 3 minutes. Add the chicken strips, stock and rice wine, bring to the boil and simmer for 20 minutes. Stir in the lemon grass and kaffir lime leaves.

Bring a separate saucepan of water to the boil and add the noodles. Cook for 3 minutes, drain well, then add them to the soup. Season with salt and pepper. Cook for a further 2 minutes. Remove from the heat, ladle into individual bowls and serve hot.

coriander chicken soup

very easy	
serves 4	
15–20 minutes	
30 minutes	

ingredients

1 tbsp sunflower oil
1 garlic clove, finely chopped
6 shallots, chopped
2 spring onions, trimmed and
   finely sliced
1 tbsp grated fresh root ginger
1 small red chilli, deseeded and
   finely chopped
300 g/10½ oz skinless chicken breasts,
   cut into strips

1 litre/1¾ pints chicken stock
85 g/3 oz fresh oyster
   mushrooms, sliced
1 tbsp Thai fish sauce
1 tbsp grated lemon rind
2 tbsp lemon juice
35 g/1¼ oz fresh coriander, chopped
1 tbsp fresh lemon grass, finely chopped
salt and pepper
175 g/6 oz beansprouts

Heat the oil in a wok or large saucepan. Add the garlic and cook over a medium heat, stirring, for 1 minute, then add the shallots, spring onions, ginger and chilli and cook, stirring, for a further 3 minutes. Add the chicken strips, stock and mushrooms, and bring to the boil. Lower the heat and stir in the fish sauce and the lemon rind and juice. Simmer for 20 minutes.

Stir in the coriander and lemon grass, and season with salt and pepper. Cook for about 2 minutes, then add the beansprouts. Cook for a further minute, then remove from the heat, ladle into individual bowls and serve hot.

cock-a-leekie

		ingredients	
easy		4 leeks, trimmed	GARNISH
		1 small whole chicken, ready	12 whole cooked prunes, stoned
serves 4		for boiling	1 tbsp chopped fresh parsley
		4 rashers lean bacon	
		2 tbsp chopped fresh parsley	
15–20 minutes		1 tbsp chopped fresh thyme	
		1 bay leaf	
		1.5 litres/2¾ pints water	
		salt and pepper	
3 hours		200 ml/7 fl oz double cream	

Chop the leeks and put them into a large pot with the chicken, bacon, herbs and water. Season with salt and pepper. Bring to the boil, then lower the heat, cover the pan and simmer for about 2¾ hours, topping up the water level when necessary.

Remove from the heat and strain the soup into a large bowl. Remove the flesh from the chicken, cut into strips and add to the bowl. Discard the carcass. Cut the bacon into strips and add to the bowl with the chicken meat. Return the soup to the pot, bring back to the boil, then lower the heat and simmer for 15 minutes. Stir in the cream and warm through gently, then remove from the heat and ladle into individual bowls. Garnish with whole prunes and chopped parsley and serve.

chicken & prawn laksa

		ingredients	
very easy		1 tbsp sesame oil	2 tbsp chopped fresh coriander
		3 spring onions, trimmed and sliced	salt and pepper
serves 4		2 tbsp Thai red curry paste	225 g/8 oz vermicelli
		1 tbsp cornflour	200 g/7 oz cooked prawns, peeled
		2 tbsp coconut milk	350 ml/12 fl oz evaporated milk
15 minutes		450 ml/16 fl oz chicken stock	175 g/6 oz beansprouts
		325 g/11½ oz skinless chicken breasts, cut into strips	chopped fresh coriander, to garnish
30 minutes			

Heat the oil in a wok or large saucepan. Add the spring onions and cook, stirring, for 2 minutes. Add the curry paste and cook for a further minute. Stir in the cornflour and coconut milk, then add the stock, chicken strips and coriander. Season with salt and pepper. Bring to the boil, then lower the heat, cover the pan and simmer for 20 minutes.

About halfway through the cooking time, bring a saucepan of lightly salted water to the boil and add the vermicelli. Cook over a medium heat for about 10 minutes if using dried pasta, or 4 minutes if using fresh (check the packet instructions), until tender but still firm to the bite. Remove from the heat, drain and divide between 4 soup bowls. Add the prawns and evaporated milk to the chicken mixture and cook for 1 minute. Add the beansprouts, cook for a further minute, then remove from the heat. Ladle the mixture over the vermicelli, garnish with coriander and serve hot.

breadcrumbed chicken morsels

		ingredients	
very easy		85 g/3 oz fresh white or wholemeal breadcrumbs	1 tbsp lemon juice
		3 tbsp grated pecorino cheese	2 tbsp chopped fresh chives
serves 4		1 tbsp dried mixed herbs	1 garlic clove, finely chopped
		salt and pepper	1 tbsp capers, chopped
		1 egg	2 shallots, finely chopped
20 minutes		4 skinless chicken breasts, cut into thick strips	50 g/1¾ oz gherkins, chopped
			6 black olives, stoned and finely chopped
30 minutes		TARTARE SAUCE 200 ml/7fl oz mayonnaise	wedges of lemon, to garnish fresh mixed salad leaves, to serve

Preheat the oven to 200°C/400°F/Gas Mark 6. Put the breadcrumbs into a large, shallow bowl. Add the pecorino cheese and mixed herbs and season well with salt and pepper. Mix together well. Beat the egg in a separate bowl. Dip the chicken strips into the beaten egg, then coat them in the breadcrumb mixture. Arrange on a baking sheet, then transfer to the preheated oven. Bake for 30 minutes until golden.

Meanwhile, to make the tartare sauce, put the mayonnaise into a bowl and stir in the lemon juice and chives. Add the garlic, capers, shallots, gherkins and olives and mix together well.

Arrange the mixed salad leaves on a large serving platter. Remove the chicken from the oven and arrange over the salad leaves. Garnish with lemon wedges and serve with the tartare sauce.

chicken crostini

		ingredients	

	very easy	12 slices French bread or rustic bread
		4 tbsp olive oil
		2 garlic cloves, chopped
		2 tbsp finely chopped fresh oregano
		salt and pepper
		100 g/3½ oz cold roast chicken, cut
		    into small, thin slices
			4 tomatoes, sliced
			12 thin slices of goat's cheese
			12 black olives, stoned and chopped
			
			fresh red and green salad leaves,
			    to serve

	serves 4		
	15 minutes		
	10 minutes		

Preheat the oven to 180°C/350°F/Gas Mark 4 and the grill to medium. Put the bread under the preheated grill and lightly toast on both sides. Meanwhile, pour the olive oil into a bowl and add the garlic and oregano. Season with salt and pepper and mix well. Remove the toasted bread slices from the grill and brush them on one side only with the oil mixture.

Place the bread slices, oiled sides up, on a baking sheet. Put some sliced chicken on top of each one, followed by a slice of tomato. Divide the slices of goat's cheese between them, then top with the chopped olives. Drizzle over the remaining oil mixture and transfer to the preheated oven. Bake for about 5 minutes, or until the cheese is golden and starting to melt. Remove from the oven and serve on a bed of fresh red and green salad leaves.

spicy chicken dippers

	ingredients	
very easy	85 g/3 oz fresh white or wholemeal breadcrumbs 3 tbsp freshly grated Parmesan cheese 1 tsp chilli powder salt and pepper 1 egg 4 skinless chicken breasts, cut into thick strips	1 tbsp tomato purée 1 small red chilli, deseeded and finely chopped 1 large tomato, deseeded and finely chopped 2 tbsp finely chopped peeled cucumber
serves 4		cherry tomatoes, halved, to garnish
15–20 minutes	SPICY TOMATO DIP 100 g/3½ oz fromage frais	TO SERVE fresh green salad leaves celery and carrots, cut into thick sticks
30 minutes		

Preheat the oven to 200°C/400°F/Gas Mark 6. Put the breadcrumbs into a large, shallow bowl. Add the Parmesan and chilli powder, season with salt and pepper and mix well. Beat the egg in a separate bowl. Dip the chicken strips into the egg, then coat them in the breadcrumb mixture. Arrange on a baking sheet and transfer to the preheated oven. Bake for 30 minutes until golden.

Meanwhile, to make the dip, put the fromage frais into a bowl and stir in the tomato purée. Add the chilli, tomato and cucumber and mix together well.

Arrange the salad leaves on a large serving platter. Remove the chicken from the oven and arrange over the salad leaves. Garnish with cherry tomatoes and serve with the celery and carrot sticks and the spicy tomato dip.

chicken livers in
red wine & thyme

	ingredients	
extremely easy	250 g/9 oz fresh chicken livers	TO SERVE
	3 tbsp lemon-flavoured oil	rocket leaves
serves 4	2 garlic cloves, finely chopped	fresh crusty bread
	4 tbsp red wine	
	1 tbsp chopped fresh thyme	
10 minutes	salt and pepper	
	sprigs of fresh thyme, to garnish	
5 minutes		

Rinse the chicken livers under cold running water and pat dry with kitchen paper. Heat the lemon-flavoured oil in a frying pan. Add the garlic and cook, stirring, over a medium heat for 2 minutes. Add the chicken livers, wine and thyme. Season with salt and pepper and cook for 3 minutes.

Meanwhile, arrange the rocket leaves on a large serving platter. Remove the pan from the heat and spoon the chicken livers over the bed of rocket. Pour over the cooking juices, then garnish with sprigs of fresh thyme and serve with fresh crusty bread.

salads & light meals

This section is crammed with delicious salads, snacks and light meals to tempt the taste buds. From Chicken, Cheese & Rocket salad to mouthwatering Buttered Chicken Parcels, and from Chicken with Creamy Spaghetti to Chicken in Cranberry & Red Wine Sauce, these dishes will be irresistible. In fact, if you find that there is never enough of these lighter dishes to go round, why not serve them as a main course? Just add some substantial accompaniments, such as crusty bread or freshly cooked rice or potatoes, and you will have a complete and satisfying meal.

thai-style chicken salad

		ingredients	
extremely easy		400 g/14 oz small new potatoes, scrubbed and halved lengthways	DRESSING
		200 g/7 oz baby corn cobs, sliced	6 tbsp chilli oil or sesame oil
serves 4		150 g/5½ oz beansprouts	2 tbsp lime juice
		3 spring onions, trimmed and sliced	1 tbsp light soy sauce
		4 cooked, skinless chicken	1 tbsp chopped fresh coriander
15 minutes		breasts, sliced	1 small, red chilli, deseeded and
		1 tbsp chopped lemon grass	finely chopped
		2 tbsp chopped fresh coriander	GARNISH
20 minutes		salt and pepper	wedges of lime
			fresh coriander leaves

Bring two saucepans of water to the boil. Put the potatoes into one saucepan and cook for 15 minutes until tender. Put the corn cobs into the other saucepan and cook for 5 minutes until tender. Drain the potatoes and corn cobs well and leave to cool.

When the vegetables are cool, transfer them into a large serving dish. Add the beansprouts, spring onions, chicken, lemon grass and coriander and season with salt and pepper.

To make the dressing, put all the ingredients into a screw-top jar and shake well. Alternatively, put them into a bowl and mix together well. Drizzle the dressing over the salad and garnish with lime wedges and coriander leaves. Serve at once.

chicken, cheese & rocket salad

extremely easy	
serves 4	
15 minutes	
—	

ingredients

150 g/5½ oz rocket leaves
2 celery sticks, trimmed and sliced
½ cucumber, sliced
2 spring onions, trimmed and sliced
2 tbsp chopped fresh parsley
25 g/1 oz walnut pieces
350 g/12 oz boneless roast
  chicken, sliced
125 g/4½ oz Stilton cheese, cubed

handful of seedless red grapes,
  halved (optional)
salt and pepper

DRESSING
2 tbsp olive oil
1 tbsp sherry vinegar
1 tsp Dijon mustard
1 tbsp chopped mixed herbs

Wash the rocket leaves, pat dry with kitchen paper and put them into a large salad bowl. Add the celery, cucumber, spring onions, parsley and walnuts and mix together well. Transfer onto a large serving platter. Arrange the chicken slices over the salad, then scatter over the cheese. Add the red grapes, if using. Season well with salt and pepper.

To make the dressing, put all the ingredients into a screw-top jar and shake well. Alternatively, put them into a bowl and mix together well. Drizzle the dressing over the salad and serve.

sage & onion drumsticks

		ingredients	
	very easy	6 tbsp butter	8 large chicken drumsticks
		1 onion, finely chopped	2 eggs, beaten
	serves 4	1 garlic clove, finely chopped	3 tbsp vegetable oil
		125 g/4½ oz fresh white or wholemeal breadcrumbs	GARNISH
		2 tbsp finely chopped fresh sage	wedges of lemon
	25 minutes	1 tbsp lemon juice	sprigs of fresh flat-leaved parsley
		salt and pepper	
	55 minutes		fresh green salad, to serve

Preheat the oven to 200°C/400°F/Gas Mark 6. Melt the butter in a frying pan over a medium heat. Add the onion and garlic and cook, stirring, for 3 minutes. Remove from the heat and stir in the breadcrumbs, sage and lemon juice. Season well with salt and pepper. Transfer to a large bowl.

Rinse the drumsticks and pat dry with kitchen paper. Turn the drumsticks in the beaten egg, then cover them in the sage and onion mixture by pressing it around them. Arrange them in a shallow roasting tin, drizzle over the oil, then roast them in the preheated oven for about 50 minutes until golden and crispy and cooked right through. If they start to brown too quickly, cover the roasting tin with foil. Remove from the oven and pile onto a serving platter. Garnish with lemon wedges and sprigs of fresh flat-leaved parsley and serve with a fresh green salad. Alternatively, to serve cold, leave to cool, cover with clingfilm and refrigerate until required.

buttered chicken parcels

		ingredients	
easy		4 tbsp butter	1 tbsp chopped fresh oregano
		4 shallots, finely chopped	pepper
serves 4		300 g/10½ oz frozen spinach, defrosted	4 large, skinless chicken breasts
		450 g/1 lb blue cheese, such as	8 slices Parma ham
		Stilton, crumbled	fresh chives, to garnish
15–20 minutes + 10 minutes to cool		1 egg, lightly beaten	
		1 tbsp chopped fresh chives	baby spinach leaves, to serve
35 minutes			

Melt half of the butter in a frying pan over a medium heat. Add the shallots and cook, stirring, for 4 minutes. Remove from the heat and leave to cool for 10 minutes.

Preheat the oven to 180°C/350°F/Gas Mark 4. Using your hands, squeeze out as much moisture from the defrosted spinach as possible. Transfer the spinach into a large bowl, add the shallots, cheese, egg, herbs and seasoning. Mix together well.

Halve each chicken breast and pound lightly to flatten each piece. Spoon some cheese mixture into the centre of each piece, then roll them up. Wrap each roll in a slice of Parma ham and secure with a cocktail stick. Transfer to a roasting dish, dot with the remaining butter and bake in the preheated oven for 30 minutes until golden.

Divide the baby spinach leaves between 4 serving plates. Remove the chicken from the oven and place 2 chicken rolls on each bed of spinach. Garnish with fresh chives and serve.

crispy coated chicken breasts

	ingredients	
easy	SWEET POTATO WEDGES	2 tbsp freshly grated pecorino cheese
	4 large sweet potatoes, peeled and	1 tbsp chopped fresh parsley
serves 4	cut into wedges	salt and pepper
	4 tbsp vegetable oil	4 skinless chicken breasts
	1 tsp chilli powder	1 egg, beaten
15–20		4 tbsp vegetable oil
minutes	50 g/1¾ oz hazelnuts, toasted	
	and ground	sprigs of fresh flat-leaved parsley,
	25 g/1 oz dried white or	to garnish
45–55	wholemeal breadcrumbs	
minutes		wedges of lemon, to serve

Preheat the oven to 200°C/400°F/Gas Mark 6. To make the potato wedges, bring a large saucepan of water to the boil. Add the potatoes, cook over a medium heat for 5 minutes, then drain. Pour 2 tablespoons of the oil into a bowl and stir in the chilli powder. Add the potatoes and turn in the mixture until coated. Transfer to a baking sheet, drizzle over the remaining oil and bake for 35–40 minutes, turning frequently, until golden and cooked through.

About 15 minutes before the end of the cooking time, put the hazelnuts, breadcrumbs, cheese and parsley into a bowl, season and mix. Dip the chicken breasts into the egg, then coat in the breadcrumb mixture. Heat the oil in a frying pan. Add the chicken and cook over a medium heat for 3–4 minutes on each side until golden. Lift out and drain on kitchen paper. Remove the potatoes from the oven, divide between 4 serving plates, and add a chicken breast to each. Garnish with parsley and serve with lemon wedges.

chicken kiev

		ingredients	
easy		4 tbsp butter, softened	3 tbsp freshly grated Parmesan cheese
		1 garlic clove, finely chopped	1 egg, beaten
serves 4		1 tbsp finely chopped fresh parsley	
		1 tbsp finely chopped fresh oregano	GARNISH
		salt and pepper	slices of lemon
		4 skinless chicken breasts	sprigs of fresh flat-leaved parsley
20 minutes		250 ml/9 fl oz vegetable oil, for	
		deep-frying	TO SERVE
		85 g/3 oz fresh white or	freshly cooked new potatoes
5 minutes		wholemeal breadcrumbs	selection of cooked vegetables

Put the butter and garlic into a bowl and mix together well. Stir in the chopped herbs and season well with salt and pepper. Pound the chicken breasts to flatten them, then put a tablespoon of herb butter in the centre of each one. Fold in the sides to enclose the butter, then secure with cocktail sticks.

Pour oil into a deep-fat fryer to a depth that will cover the chicken parcels. Heat until very hot. Meanwhile, combine the breadcrumbs and grated Parmesan on a plate. Dip the chicken parcels into the beaten egg, then coat in the breadcrumb mixture. Transfer the chicken to the hot oil and deep-fry for 5 minutes, or until cooked through. Lift out the chicken and drain on kitchen paper. Divide the chicken between 4 serving plates, garnish with lemon slices and sprigs of fresh flat-leaved parsley and serve with new potatoes and a selection of vegetables.

chicken & peanut stir-fry

		ingredients	
very easy		2 tbsp groundnut oil	150 g/5½ oz sugar snap peas, trimmed
		1 garlic clove, chopped	125 g/4½ oz baby corn cobs
serves 4		3 spring onions, trimmed and sliced	2 tbsp smooth peanut butter
		4 skinless chicken breasts, cut into	1 tbsp light soy sauce
		bite-sized chunks	
		1 tbsp grated fresh root ginger	TO SERVE
15 minutes		½ tsp chilli powder	freshly cooked brown or white rice
			fresh green salad
8–9 minutes			

Heat the oil in a preheated wok or large frying pan. Add the garlic and spring onions and stir-fry over a medium-high heat for 1 minute. Add the chicken pieces, ginger and chilli powder and stir-fry for a further 4 minutes. Add the sugar snap peas and baby corn cobs and cook for 2 minutes.

In a bowl, mix together the peanut butter and soy sauce, then add it to the wok. Stir-fry for a further minute. Remove from the heat, pile onto 4 serving plates and serve with freshly cooked rice and a fresh green salad.

five-spice chicken
with vegetables

		ingredients	
very easy		2 tbsp sesame oil	1 tbsp grated fresh root ginger
		1 garlic clove, chopped	125 ml/4 fl oz chicken stock
serves 4		3 spring onions, trimmed and sliced	100 g/3½ oz baby corn cobs, sliced
		1 tbsp cornflour	300 g/10½ oz beansprouts
		2 tbsp rice wine	
15 minutes		4 skinless chicken breasts, cut	finely chopped spring onion, to
		into strips	garnish (optional)
		1 tbsp Chinese five-spice powder	freshly cooked jasmine rice, to serve
9–10 minutes			

Heat the oil in a preheated wok or large frying pan. Add the garlic and the sliced spring onions and stir-fry over a medium-high heat for 1 minute.

In a bowl, mix together the cornflour and rice wine, then add the mixture to the pan. Stir-fry for 1 minute, then add the chicken, five-spice powder, ginger and stock and cook for a further 4 minutes. Add the corn cobs and cook for 2 minutes, then add the beansprouts and cook for a further minute.

Remove from the heat, garnish with chopped spring onions, if using, and serve with freshly cooked jasmine rice.

chicken with creamy spaghetti

		ingredients	
very easy		MARINADE	450 g/1 lb spaghetti
		2 tbsp olive oil	salt and pepper
		6 tbsp white wine	2 tbsp olive oil
serves 4		1 garlic clove, chopped	6 tbsp soured cream
		1 tbsp chopped fresh thyme	1 tbsp chopped fresh thyme
10–15 minutes + 3 hours to marinate		1 tbsp chopped fresh rosemary	
			GARNISH
		4 skinless chicken breasts, cut	freshly grated Parmesan cheese
		into strips	sprigs of fresh rosemary
8–16 minutes			

To make the marinade, put all the ingredients into a large, shallow, glass dish and mix together well. Add the chicken and coat in the marinade. Cover with clingfilm and refrigerate for 3 hours.

Bring a saucepan of lightly salted water to the boil and add the spaghetti. Cook over a medium heat for 10 minutes if using dried pasta, or 4 minutes if using fresh (check the packet instructions), until tender but firm to the bite. Meanwhile, lift the chicken out of the marinade, drain, and season. Discard the marinade. Heat the oil in a frying pan, add the chicken and cook over a medium heat for 2–3 minutes on each side, or until cooked through.

In a bowl, mix the soured cream with the thyme. Drain the spaghetti and mix with half of the soured cream. Pile the spaghetti onto a large serving platter, then top with the chicken. Pour over the remaining soured cream, scatter over the Parmesan, garnish with rosemary sprigs and serve.

lemon chicken with rice

		ingredients	
very easy		MARINADE	1 garlic clove, chopped
		juice and grated rind of 1 lemon	1 onion, thinly sliced
serves 4		2 garlic cloves, chopped	juice and grated rind of 1 lemon
		3 tbsp lemon oil	125 ml/4 fl oz chicken stock
		6 tbsp white wine	
10–15 minutes + 3 hours to marinate		1 tbsp chopped fresh coriander	GARNISH
			toasted flaked almonds
		4 skinless chicken breasts, cut into	fresh coriander leaves
		bite-sized chunks	
		salt and pepper	TO SERVE
10 minutes		4 tbsp butter	freshly cooked rice
			selection of freshly cooked vegetables

To make the marinade, put all the ingredients into a large, shallow, glass dish and mix together well. Add the chicken and coat in the marinade. Cover with clingfilm and refrigerate for 3 hours.

Lift out the chicken, drain well and season. Discard the marinade. Heat the butter in a frying pan, add the garlic and onion and cook over a low heat, stirring, for 2 minutes. Add the lemon juice and rind, stock and chicken and bring to the boil. Lower the heat to medium and cook for 7–8 minutes, or until cooked through.

Arrange the cooked rice on a large serving platter. Remove the pan from the heat and place the chicken mixture over the rice. Scatter over the almonds and coriander leaves. Serve with a selection of freshly cooked vegetables.

chicken in cranberry
& red wine sauce

		ingredients	
	easy	LEMON POTATOES	1 bay leaf
		600 g/1 lb 5 oz small new	salt and pepper
	serves 4	potatoes, scrubbed	
		2 garlic cloves, chopped	CRANBERRY & RED WINE SAUCE
		3 tbsp olive oil	175 g/6 oz fresh cranberries
		juice of $\frac{1}{2}$ lemon	100 g/3$\frac{1}{2}$ oz caster sugar
	20 minutes	1 tbsp chopped fresh thyme	300 ml/10 fl oz red wine
		salt and pepper	
			sprigs of fresh thyme, to garnish
	1 hour	300 ml/10 fl oz chicken stock	
	25 minutes	4 skinless, boneless chicken breasts	

Preheat the oven to 200°C/400°F/Gas Mark 6. Arrange the potatoes in a roasting tin. Put the garlic, oil, lemon juice and thyme into a bowl, season and mix well. Pour over the potatoes and turn in the mixture until thoroughly coated. Roast in the preheated oven for 50 minutes, basting occasionally, until golden brown and tender.

Halfway through the cooking time, pour the stock into a saucepan and bring to the boil. Add the chicken and bay leaf, and season with salt and pepper. Reduce the heat and simmer for about 20 minutes until cooked through.

To make the sauce, put all the ingredients into a saucepan and bring to the boil. Reduce the heat and simmer, stirring occasionally, for 15 minutes until thickened. Lift out the chicken and discard the bay leaf. Slice the chicken and arrange on 4 serving plates. Remove the potatoes from the oven and divide between the plates. Spoon over the sauce, garnish with thyme and serve.

sweet & sour chicken

		ingredients	
very easy		4 skinless chicken breasts	1 tsp chilli powder
		salt and pepper	125 ml/4 fl oz orange juice
serves 4		75 g/2¾ oz plain flour	4 tbsp lime juice
		2 tbsp olive oil	
		2 large garlic cloves, chopped	TO GARNISH
		1 bay leaf	toasted flaked almonds
15 minutes		1 tbsp grated fresh root ginger	wedges of lime
		1 tbsp chopped fresh lemon grass	
		4 tbsp sherry vinegar	TO SERVE
40–45 minutes		5 tbsp rice wine or sherry	sautéed sliced potatoes
		1 tbsp clear honey	carrots, cut into sticks and
			freshly cooked

Season the chicken breasts on both sides with salt and pepper, then roll them in the flour until coated. Heat the olive oil in a large frying pan. Add the garlic and cook, stirring, over a medium heat for 1 minute. Add the chicken, bay leaf, ginger and lemon grass and cook for 2 minutes on each side.

Add the vinegar, rice wine and honey, bring to the boil, then lower the heat and simmer, stirring occasionally, for 10 minutes. Add the chilli powder, then stir in the orange juice and lime juice. Simmer for a further 10 minutes. Using a slotted spoon, lift out the chicken and reserve. Strain and reserve the liquid and discard the bay leaf, then return the liquid to the pan with the chicken. Simmer for a further 15–20 minutes.

Remove from the heat and transfer to individual serving plates. Garnish with toasted flaked almonds and lime wedges, and serve with sautéed sliced potatoes and freshly cooked carrots.

stuffed chicken breasts
with herbs

		ingredients	
easy		4 tbsp butter	salt and pepper
		1 onion, finely chopped	4 large, skinless chicken breasts
serves 4		4 rashers smoked lean back bacon, chopped	TO GARNISH
		450 g/1 lb Gruyère cheese, grated	toasted pine kernels
		1 egg, lightly beaten	sprigs of fresh basil
15 minutes		1 tbsp chopped fresh sage	
		2 tbsp chopped fresh basil	freshly cooked paglia e fieno, or other pasta ribbons, to serve
35 minutes			

Preheat the oven to 180°C/350°F/Gas Mark 4. Melt half of the butter in a frying pan over a medium heat. Add the onion and cook, stirring, for 2 minutes. Add the bacon and cook for a further 2 minutes. Remove from the heat and transfer to a large bowl. Add the cheese, egg and herbs to the bowl. Season with salt and pepper and mix together well.

Halve each chicken breast and pound lightly to flatten each piece. Spoon some bacon mixture into the centre of each piece, roll up and secure with cocktail sticks. Transfer to a large roasting dish and dot with the remaining butter. Bake in the preheated oven for 30 minutes until golden.

Divide the freshly cooked pasta between 4 serving plates. Remove the chicken from the oven and place 2 chicken rolls on top of each bed of pasta. Garnish with toasted pine kernels and sprigs of fresh basil and serve.

main courses

Chicken is popular in cookery all over the world. This section presents a spectacular array of exciting and satisfying dishes from different countries, such as Italian Pesto Chicken, and Coq au Vin from France. There is also a Fiery Chicken Vindaloo, which takes its inspiration from India. And what could demonstrate chicken's wonderful versatility better than Mexican Chicken with Chilli Chocolate Sauce? Mexican cooks have been pairing rich chocolate with hot chillies for centuries, and the flavour of chicken complements this combination perfectly.

roast chicken with hazelnut stuffing

	ingredients	

easy	3 tbsp butter, softened
	1 garlic clove, finely chopped
	3 tbsp finely chopped
	    toasted hazelnuts
	1 tbsp grated lemon rind
	1 tbsp chopped fresh
	    flat-leaved parsley
	salt and pepper
	1 medium oven-ready chicken,
	    about 1.8 kg/4 lb
	1 lemon, cut into quarters
		1 tbsp olive oil
		425 ml/15 fl oz sherry
		1 tsp ground cumin
		1 heaped tsp cornflour
		
		TO GARNISH
		slices of lemon
		sprigs of fresh flat-leaved parsley
		
		TO SERVE
		roast potatoes
		selection of freshly cooked vegetables

serves 4

15 minutes
+ 10 minutes
to rest

1 hour
45 minutes

Preheat the oven to 190°C/375°F/Gas Mark 5. Mix 1 tablespoon of the butter with the garlic, hazelnuts, lemon rind and parsley. Season well. Loosen the chicken skin from the breast without breaking it. Push the butter mixture evenly between the skin and breast meat. Put the lemon quarters inside the body cavity.

Pour the oil into a roasting tin. Put the chicken in it. Pour over the sherry, season, rub the skin with cumin and dot with the remaining butter. Roast for 1 hour 40 minutes, basting occasionally, until cooked through. Check it is cooked by inserting a knife into the thickest part of a thigh – the juices should run clear. Lift out and place on a serving platter to rest for 10 minutes. Mix the cornflour with 2 tablespoons of water, then stir into the juices in the tin. Transfer to the hob. Stir over a low heat until thickened. Add more water if necessary. Garnish the chicken with lemon slices and parsley. Serve with roast potatoes, vegetables and the cooking sauce.

honey-glazed chicken

easy	
serves 4	
15 minutes + 10 minutes to rest	
1 hour 45 minutes	

ingredients

3 tbsp clear honey
½ tsp salt
1 tsp dried mustard
1 tbsp light soy sauce
1 tbsp olive oil
1 medium oven-ready chicken, about 1.8 kg/4 lb
1 orange, cut into quarters

150 ml/5 fl oz chicken stock
1 tsp cornflour
150 ml/5 fl oz red wine
150 ml/5 fl oz single cream

seedless red grapes, halved, to garnish

freshly cooked mixed white rice and wild rice, to serve

Preheat the oven to 190°C/375°F/Gas Mark 5. Put the honey, salt, mustard and soy sauce into a bowl and mix well. Pour the oil into a roasting tin and put the chicken in it. Put the orange quarters inside the body cavity. Pour over the stock, then spread over the honey mixture. Roast for 1 hour 40 minutes, basting occasionally, until golden and cooked through. To check it is cooked, insert a knife into a thickest part of a thigh – the juices should run clear. Lift out the chicken and leave to rest for 10 minutes.

Mix the cornflour with 1–2 tablespoons of water, then stir into the juices in the roasting tin. Transfer to the hob and stir over a low heat for 1 minute, then pour in the wine. Bring to the boil, lower the heat and cook, stirring, for 1 minute. Remove from the heat and stir in the cream. Arrange the cooked mixed rice on a serving platter, then place the chicken on it. Garnish with grape halves and serve with the red wine sauce.

herb chicken with
white wine & vegetables

easy	
serves 4	
15 minutes + 10 minutes to rest	
1 hour 45 minutes	

ingredients

2 garlic cloves, finely chopped
1 tbsp chopped fresh
   flat-leaved parsley
1 tbsp chopped fresh thyme
salt and pepper
1 medium oven-ready chicken,
   about 1.8 kg/4 lb
2 shallots, halved
1 lemon, cut into quarters

1 bay leaf
1 tbsp olive oil
300 ml/10 fl oz white wine
1 tbsp cornflour

sprigs of fresh thyme, to garnish

TO SERVE
roast potatoes
selection of freshly cooked vegetables
gravy

Preheat the oven to 190°C/375°F/Gas Mark 5. Put the garlic, parsley and thyme into a bowl and mix well. Season well. Loosen the chicken skin from the breast without breaking it. Push the mixture evenly between the skin and breast meat. Put the shallot halves, lemon quarters and bay leaf inside the body cavity.

Pour the oil into a roasting tin and place the chicken in it. Pour over half of the wine. Roast for 1 hour 40 minutes, basting occasionally, until golden and cooked through. Check it is cooked by inserting a knife into the thickest part of a thigh – the juices should run clear. Lift out the chicken. Leave to rest for 10 minutes.

Mix the cornflour with 1–2 tablespoons of water, then stir into the juices in the tin. Transfer to the hob and stir over a low heat for 1 minute. Stir in the remaining wine. Bring to the boil, lower the heat and cook, stirring, for 1 minute. Cut the chicken into slices, garnish with thyme and serve with roast potatoes, vegetables and gravy.

italian pesto chicken

		ingredients	

very easy	PESTO
	25 g/1 oz fresh basil, stalks removed
	150 g/5½ oz pine kernels
	3 garlic cloves, roughly chopped
	100 ml/3½ fl oz extra-virgin olive oil
	75 g/2¾ oz Parmesan cheese,
	  freshly grated
	salt and pepper
		75 g/2¾ oz sun-dried tomatoes in olive
		  oil, drained and chopped
		2 tbsp extra-virgin olive oil
		125 ml/4 fl oz white wine
		200 g/7 oz canned chopped tomatoes
		
		GARNISH
		black olives, stoned and halved
		sprigs of fresh basil

serves 4			
15–20 minutes			
30 minutes	4 skinless chicken breasts 8 slices Parma ham	freshly cooked linguine, to serve	

Preheat the oven to 180°C/350°F/Gas Mark 4. To make the pesto, put all the ingredients into a food processor and season with salt and pepper. Blend for a few seconds until smooth.

Halve each chicken breast and pound lightly to flatten each piece. Spread on one side only with pesto, then top with the Parma ham. Add a tablespoon of sun-dried tomatoes to each one, then roll them up and secure with cocktail sticks.

Pour the olive oil into a large roasting tin. Arrange the chicken in the tin, then pour over the wine. Add the chopped tomatoes and bake in the preheated oven for 30 minutes.

Stir any remaining pesto into the cooked pasta and arrange on 4 serving plates. Remove the chicken from the oven, discard the cocktail stick and slice the chicken in half, widthways. Divide between the plates. Pour over some of the cooking sauce, garnish with halved black olives and sprigs of basil and serve.

fiery chicken vindaloo

		ingredients	
	very easy	1 tsp ground cumin	bite-sized chunks
		1 tsp ground cinnamon	2 small red chillies, deseeded
	serves 4	2 tsp dried mustard	and chopped
		1½ tsp ground coriander	450 g/1 lb potatoes, peeled and cut
		1 tsp cayenne pepper	into chunks
		5 tbsp red wine vinegar	800 g/1 lb 12 oz canned
	15 minutes	1 tsp brown sugar	chopped tomatoes
		150 ml/5 fl oz vegetable oil	1 tbsp tomato purée
		8 garlic cloves, crushed	a few drops of red food colouring
	1 hour	3 red onions, sliced	salt and pepper
	10 minutes	4 skinless chicken breasts, cut into	freshly boiled rice, to serve

Put the cumin, cinnamon, mustard, ground coriander and cayenne pepper into a bowl. Add the vinegar and sugar and mix well.

Heat the oil in a large frying pan. Add the garlic and onions and cook, stirring, over a medium heat for 5 minutes. Add the chicken and cook for a further 3 minutes, then add the chillies, potatoes, chopped tomatoes and tomato purée, and a few drops of red food colouring. Stir in the spice mixture, season generously with salt and pepper and bring to the boil. Lower the heat, cover the pan and simmer, stirring occasionally, for 1 hour.

Arrange the cooked rice on a large serving platter. Remove the pan from the heat, spoon the chicken mixture over the rice and serve.

mexican chicken with chilli chocolate sauce

		ingredients	
very easy		2 tbsp chilli oil	500 ml/18 fl oz chicken stock
		1 garlic clove, chopped	50 g/1¾ oz raisins
serves 4		4 skinless chicken breasts	50 g/1¾ oz pine kernels
		1 onion, chopped	1 tsp ground mixed spice
		1 red pepper, skinned, deseeded	1 tsp brown sugar
		and chopped	50 g/1¾ oz dark chocolate, broken into
15–20 minutes		1 large tomato, skinned, deseeded	small pieces
		and chopped	100 ml/3½ fl oz red wine
		1 small red chilli, deseeded	juice of ½ orange
1 hour		and chopped	freshly cooked rice or potatoes, to serve
		1 tbsp cocoa powder	

Heat the oil in a flameproof casserole. Add the garlic and cook, stirring, over a medium heat for 3 minutes. Add the chicken and cook for 3 minutes, then turn over and cook on the other side for a further 2 minutes. Lift out the chicken, cut into bite-sized chunks, and reserve.

Preheat the oven to 180°C/350°F/Gas Mark 4. Add the onion, red pepper, tomato, chilli and cocoa powder to the pan. Cook, stirring, for 5 minutes. Then add the stock, raisins, pine kernels, mixed spice and sugar and cook for 2 minutes. Return the chicken to the casserole. Add the chocolate and stir until melted, then stir in the red wine and orange juice. Bring to the boil then remove from the heat.

Transfer to the preheated oven and bake for about 40 minutes or until cooked through. Remove from the oven and serve with freshly cooked rice or potatoes.

sweet chicken pie

		ingredients	
easy		**PASTRY**	25 g/1 oz raisins
		350 g/12 oz plain flour, plus extra for dusting	50 g/1¾ oz hazelnuts, toasted and ground
serves 4		pinch of salt	50 g/1¾ oz Cheddar cheese, grated
		175 g/6 oz butter, chopped, plus extra for greasing	1 tsp ground mixed spice
20 minutes + 1 hour to chill		about 6 tbsp cold water	salt and pepper
			1 egg, lightly beaten
		250 ml/9 fl oz chicken stock	
1¼ hours		700 g/1 lb 9 oz boneless chicken, cut into bite-sized chunks	**TO SERVE**
			freshly cooked potatoes
		3 tbsp brandy	selection of freshly cooked vegetables
			seedless white grapes, halved (optional)

To make the pastry, mix the flour and salt in a bowl. Rub in the butter to form fine crumbs. Gradually mix in enough cold water to make a pliable dough. Knead lightly. Wrap in clingfilm and place in the refrigerator to chill for 1 hour. Meanwhile, pour the stock into a pan and bring to the boil. Lower the heat, add the chicken, and cook for 30 minutes. Remove from the heat, cool for 25 minutes, then transfer to a bowl, draining off any excess liquid. Stir in the remaining ingredients. Season.

Preheat the oven to 190°C/375°F/Gas Mark 5. Grease a 23-cm/9-inch pie dish with butter. Remove the dough from the refrigerator. On a floured surface, shape half into a ball, roll out to a thickness of 5 mm/ ¼ inch and use it to line the dish. Spoon in the chicken filling, then roll out the remaining pastry. Moisten the pie rim with water, cover the pie with the remaining pastry and trim the edges. Cut 2 slits in the top and add pastry leaf shapes made from trimmings. Brush with the egg. Bake for 45 minutes. Serve with potatoes and vegetables.

coq au vin

very easy	
serves 4	
15 minutes	
1 hour 10 minutes	

ingredients

2 tbsp butter
8 baby onions
125 g/4½ oz streaky bacon,
    roughly chopped
4 fresh chicken joints
1 garlic clove, finely chopped
12 button mushrooms
300 ml/10 fl oz red wine

1 bouquet garni
1 tbsp chopped fresh tarragon
salt and pepper
2 tsp cornflour

sprigs of fresh flat-leaved parsley,
    to garnish

sautéed sliced potatoes, to serve

Melt half of the butter in a large frying pan over a medium heat. Add the onions and bacon and cook, stirring, for 3 minutes. Lift out the bacon and onions and reserve. Melt the remaining butter in the pan and add the chicken. Cook for 3 minutes, then turn over and cook on the other side for 2 minutes. Drain off some of the chicken fat before returning the bacon and onions to the pan. Then add the garlic, mushrooms, red wine and herbs. Season with salt and pepper. Cook for about 1 hour, or until cooked through. Remove from the heat, lift out the chicken, onions, bacon and mushrooms, transfer them to a serving platter and keep warm. Discard the bouquet garni.

Mix the cornflour with 1–2 tablespoons of water, then stir it into the juices in the pan. Bring to the boil, lower the heat and cook, stirring, for 1 minute. Pour the sauce over the chicken, garnish with sprigs of parsley and serve with sautéed sliced potatoes.

chicken & barley stew

		ingredients	
very easy	2 tbsp vegetable oil	1 tbsp tomato purée
	8 small, skinless chicken thighs	1 bay leaf
serves 4	500 ml/18 fl oz chicken stock	1 courgette, trimmed and sliced
	100 g/3½ oz pearl barley, rinsed and drained	2 tbsp chopped fresh parsley
		2 tbsp plain flour
15 minutes	200 g/7 oz small new potatoes, scrubbed and halved lengthways	salt and pepper
	2 large carrots, peeled and sliced	sprigs of fresh flat-leaved parsley, to garnish
	1 leek, trimmed and sliced	
1 hour	2 shallots, sliced	fresh crusty bread, to serve

Heat the oil in a large pot over a medium heat. Add the chicken and cook for 3 minutes, then turn over and cook on the other side for a further 2 minutes. Add the stock, barley, potatoes, carrots, leek, shallots, tomato purée and the bay leaf. Bring to the boil, lower the heat and simmer for 30 minutes. Add the courgette and parsley, cover the pan and cook for a further 20 minutes, or until the chicken is cooked through. Remove the bay leaf and discard.

In a separate bowl, mix the flour with 4 tablespoons of water and stir into a smooth paste. Add it to the stew and cook, stirring, over a low heat for a further 5 minutes. Season. Remove from the heat, ladle into individual serving bowls and garnish with sprigs of fresh parsley. Serve with fresh crusty bread.

chicken & vegetable bake

very easy	
serves 4	
15 minutes	
1 hour	

ingredients

FILLING
300 ml/10 fl oz chicken stock
450 g/1 lb boneless chicken, chopped
100 g/3½ oz button mushrooms
1 tbsp butter, for greasing
1 tbsp cornflour
150 ml/5 fl oz milk
200 g/7 oz carrots, peeled, blanched
 and chopped
1 tbsp chopped fresh rosemary
salt and pepper

TOPPING
900 g/2 lb potatoes, peeled, cooked
 and mashed
1 onion, grated
100 g/3½ oz Cheddar cheese, grated

sprigs of fresh rosemary, to garnish

selection of freshly cooked vegetables,
 to serve

To make the filling, pour the stock into a large saucepan and bring to the boil. Add the chicken and mushrooms, lower the heat, cover the pan and simmer for 25–30 minutes. Grease a 1.2-litre/2-pint ovenproof pie dish with butter. Remove the pan from the heat, lift out the chicken and mushrooms and place in the prepared pie dish. Reserve the stock.

Preheat the oven to 200°C/400°F/Gas Mark 6. In a bowl, mix the cornflour with enough of the milk to make a smooth paste, then stir in the remaining milk. Pour the mixture into the pie dish, add the stock, then the carrots and rosemary, and season well. To make the topping, put the mashed potatoes into a bowl. Add the grated onion and half of the cheese, and mix well. Spoon the mixture over the chicken filling, level the surface, then scatter over the remaining cheese. Bake for 30 minutes until golden. Remove from the oven, garnish with rosemary and serve with vegetables.

chicken risotto

easy	
serves 4	
10–15 minutes	
45–50 minutes	

ingredients

4 tbsp butter
1 onion, chopped
125 g/4½ oz skinless chicken
  breasts, chopped
350 g/12 oz risotto rice
1 tsp turmeric
salt and pepper
300 ml/10 fl oz white wine
1.2 litre/2 pints hot chicken stock

75 g/2¾ oz chestnut
  mushrooms, sliced
50 g/1¾ oz cashew nuts, halved

TO GARNISH
shavings of fresh Parmesan cheese
fresh basil leaves

wild rocket, to serve

Melt the butter in a large saucepan over a medium heat. Add the onion and cook, stirring, for 1 minute. Add the chicken and cook, stirring, for a further 5 minutes.

Add the rice and cook, stirring, for 15 minutes. Then add the turmeric, season with salt and pepper, and mix well. Gradually stir in the wine, then stir in the hot stock, a ladleful at a time, waiting for each ladleful to be absorbed before stirring in the next. Simmer for 20 minutes, stirring from time to time, until the rice is tender and nearly all of the liquid has been absorbed. If necessary, add a little more stock to prevent the risotto drying out. Stir in the mushrooms and cashew nuts, and cook for a further 3 minutes.

Arrange the rocket on 4 individual serving plates. Remove the risotto from the heat and spoon it over the rocket. Scatter over the Parmesan shavings and basil leaves and serve at once.

entertaining

The versatility of chicken makes it the ideal food for entertaining, and this section presents a delicious range of recipes for barbecues, buffets and dinner parties. Your guests will find the Barbecued Tandoori Chicken irresistible, while the Chicken Pinwheels with Blue Cheese & Herbs will invite many admiring comments. Children will love the Crispy Chicken Burgers, and the elegant Poached Chicken with Brandy & Cream will linger in the memory long after your guests have eaten it.

barbecued tandoori chicken

	ingredients	
very easy	MARINADE	SKEWERS
	450 ml/16 fl oz natural yogurt	6 skinless chicken breasts
serves 4	4 tbsp lime juice	16 baby onions
	2 garlic cloves, crushed	1 red pepper, deseeded and chopped
	1 tsp salt	1 green pepper, deseeded and chopped
15 minutes + 2 hours to marinate	pinch of saffron threads	
	1 tsp ground coriander	GARNISH
	1 tsp ground cumin	lime wedges
	1 tsp ground ginger	fresh coriander leaves
15–20 minutes	½ tsp chilli powder	
	pepper	freshly steamed or boiled rice, to serve

To make the marinade, put the yogurt, lime juice, garlic, salt and spices into a large, shallow, non-metallic (glass or ceramic) bowl, which will not react with acid. Season with plenty of pepper and mix together well.

Cut the chicken into bite-sized pieces and thread onto 8 skewers, alternating with the onions and peppers. When the skewers are full (leave a small space at either end), put them in the bowl and turn in the marinade until well coated. Cover with clingfilm and leave in the refrigerator to marinate for at least 2 hours.

Lift the skewers out of the marinade. Barbecue over hot coals or cook under a hot grill for 15–20 minutes, or until cooked right through, turning them frequently and basting with the remaining marinade. Remove from the heat, arrange on a bed of freshly cooked rice, garnish with fresh coriander leaves and serve.

chicken pittas

		ingredients	
very easy		4 tbsp lemon juice	200 g/7 oz kalamata olives
		2 garlic cloves, crushed	
serves 4		1 tsp dried oregano	DRESSING
		1 tbsp clear honey	1 tbsp lemon juice
		1 small red chilli, deseeded and	5 tbsp extra-virgin olive oil
15–20 minutes + 2 hours to marinate		finely chopped	2 tbsp white wine vinegar
		salt and pepper	½ tsp sugar
		6 skinless chicken breasts, cut into	2 tbsp chopped fresh coriander
		bite-sized pieces	
15–20 minutes		4 tomatoes, sliced	fresh coriander leaves, to garnish
		1 red onion, sliced	8 small pitta breads, warmed, to serve

Put the lemon juice, garlic, oregano, honey and chilli into a large, shallow, non-metallic (glass or ceramic) bowl, which will not react with acid. Season with plenty of salt and pepper and mix well. Add the chicken pieces to the bowl and turn them in the marinade until they are coated. Cover with clingfilm and place in the refrigerator to marinate for at least 2 hours.

Lift the chicken breasts out of the marinade. Barbecue over hot coals or cook under a hot grill for 15–20 minutes, or until cooked right through, turning them frequently and basting with the remaining marinade. While they are cooking, make the dressing. Put all the ingredients into a screw-top jar and shake well, or put them into a bowl and mix together. Put the tomatoes, onion and olives into a separate bowl. Halve the olives and add to the tomatoes. Drizzle over the dressing. Divide between 8 split pitta breads and add the chicken. Garnish with coriander and serve.

chicken & mushroom kebabs

very easy	
serves 4	
15 minutes + 2 hours to marinate	
15–20 minutes	

ingredients

MARINADE
125 ml/4 fl oz extra-virgin olive oil
2 garlic cloves, crushed
1 tbsp dried basil
1 tbsp dried thyme
salt and pepper

6 skinless chicken breasts, cut into
   bite-sized pieces
16 button mushrooms

8 baby onions
8 cherry tomatoes

sprigs of fresh rosemary, to garnish

TO SERVE
fresh mixed salad leaves
chopped cucumber
long sprigs of fresh rosemary to use as
   skewers, optional

To make the marinade, put the oil, garlic, basil and thyme into a large, shallow bowl. Season with salt and pepper and mix well.

Thread the chicken pieces onto 8 skewers (or rosemary skewers, if using), alternating them with the mushrooms, onions and cherry tomatoes. When the skewers are full (leave a small space at either end), put them into the bowl and turn them in the marinade until they are well coated. Cover with clingfilm and place in the refrigerator to marinate for at least 2 hours.

Lift the skewers out of the marinade. Barbecue over hot coals or cook under a hot grill for 15–20 minutes, or until cooked right through, turning them frequently and basting with the remaining marinade. Remove from the heat, arrange the skewers on a bed of fresh mixed salad leaves and chopped cucumber, garnish with sprigs of fresh rosemary and serve.

sweet & sour chicken drumsticks

		ingredients	
very easy	8 chicken drumsticks	1 tsp paprika	
		salt and pepper	
	MARINADE		
serves 4	4 tbsp sherry vinegar	4 long red chillies, made into flowers	
	2 tbsp light soy sauce	(see below), to garnish	
	3 garlic cloves, crushed		
15 minutes + 2 hours to marinate	2 tbsp clear honey	rocket leaves, to serve	
	2 tbsp tomato purée		
15–20 minutes			

To make the marinade, put the vinegar, soy sauce, garlic, honey, tomato purée and paprika into a large, shallow, non-metallic (glass or ceramic) bowl, which will not react with acid. Season with salt and pepper and mix well. Add the chicken drumsticks to the bowl and turn in the marinade until well coated. Cover with clingfilm and place in the refrigerator to marinate for at least 2 hours. Meanwhile, make the chilli flowers. Using a sharp knife, make 6 slits about 1 cm/½ inch in length from the stalk end to the tip of each chilli. Put them in a bowl of iced water and soak for at least 30 minutes until they have expanded into flower shapes.

Lift the drumsticks out of the marinade. Barbecue over hot coals or cook under a hot grill for 15–20 minutes, or until cooked through, turning them frequently and basting with the remaining marinade. Arrange the rocket on a large serving platter and pile the cooked drumsticks on top. Garnish with the chilli flowers and serve.

honey-glazed chicken skewers

		ingredients	
very easy	6 skinless chicken breasts, cut into bite-sized pieces	HONEY GLAZE
		16 button mushrooms	2 tbsp white wine vinegar
serves 4	3 red onions, cut into bite-sized pieces	175 ml/6 fl oz clear honey
	2 red peppers, deseeded and cut into bite-sized pieces	1 tbsp prepared mustard
		1 tbsp soy sauce
15 minutes	2 courgettes, trimmed and cut into bite-sized pieces	2 tbsp cornflour
		fresh flat-leaved parsley, to garnish
20–25 minutes		mixture of freshly cooked white rice and wild rice, to serve

Thread the chicken pieces onto 8 skewers, alternating with the mushrooms, onions, red peppers and courgettes (leave a small space at either end).

To make the honey glaze, put the vinegar, honey, mustard and soy sauce into a small saucepan and bring to the boil. Meanwhile, in a bowl, mix the cornflour with enough water to make a smooth paste. When the honey mixture has reached boiling point, lower the heat, stir in the cornflour mixture and simmer gently for 1 minute. Remove from the heat.

Brush the honey glaze over the chicken skewers until they are well coated. Barbecue over hot coals or cook under a hot grill for 15–20 minutes, or until cooked right through, turning them frequently and basting with the remaining honey glaze. Remove from the heat, arrange on a bed of freshly cooked white rice and wild rice, garnish with fresh parsley and serve.

mexican citrus chicken

		ingredients	
very easy	4 skinless chicken breasts	2 tbsp orange juice	
		1 tbsp red wine vinegar	
	MARINADE	1 garlic clove, crushed	
serves 4	4 tbsp lime juice	6 tomatoes, roughly chopped	
	1 tbsp orange juice	3 spring onions, trimmed and sliced	
	4 tbsp extra-virgin olive oil	2 tbsp chopped fresh flat-leaved parsley	
20 minutes + 2 hours to marinate	1 small red chilli, deseeded		
	1 tbsp tequila	sprigs of fresh mint, to garnish	
	CITRUS SALSA	8 small flour tortillas, warmed, to serve	
15–20 minutes	2 tbsp lime juice		

To make the marinade, finely chop the chilli and put with the citrus juices, olive oil and tequila into a large, shallow, non-metallic (glass or ceramic) bowl, which will not react with acid. Mix well. Halve each chicken breast and pound lightly to tenderise each piece. Add them to the bowl and turn in the marinade until coated. Cover with clingfilm and place in the refrigerator to marinate for at least 2 hours.

About 30 minutes before the end of the marinating time, make the salsa. Put the lime juice, orange juice, vinegar and garlic into a large bowl and mix together. Add the tomatoes, spring onions and chopped parsley and toss together until coated. Cover with clingfilm and leave to stand for 30 minutes.

Lift the chicken out of the marinade. Barbecue over hot coals or cook under a hot grill for 15–20 minutes, or until cooked through, turning frequently and basting with marinade. Divide the chicken and salsa between 8 warmed tortillas, garnish with mint and serve.

crispy chicken burgers

	ingredients	
easy	225 g/8 oz fresh white or wholemeal breadcrumbs	1 tbsp chopped fresh thyme
	225 g/8 oz cooked chicken meat, chopped	1 tbsp chopped fresh parsley
serves 4		salt and pepper
	2 eggs	
	1 onion, roughly chopped	fresh mixed salad leaves, to garnish
15–20 minutes + 30 minutes to chill	1 small red chilli, deseeded and chopped	TO SERVE
	1 large garlic clove, chopped	hamburger buns
	1 tbsp grated lemon rind	freshly sliced onion rings and
8–10 minutes		tomatoes, cooked or raw

Put 150 g/5½ oz of the breadcrumbs into a food processor with the chicken. Add one of the eggs, then all of the onion, chilli, garlic, lemon rind, thyme and parsley. Season well with salt and pepper, then blend until smooth. Transfer into a bowl, cover with clingfilm and refrigerate for 30 minutes.

Remove from the refrigerator and, using your hands, shape the mixture into burgers. Beat the remaining egg, then dip the burgers into the egg and coat with the remaining breadcrumbs. Barbecue over hot coals or cook under a hot grill for 4–5 minutes on each side, or until cooked right through.

Remove from the heat. Serve with hamburger buns and onion rings and tomatoes, garnished with salad leaves.

chicken pinwheels
with blue cheese & herbs

		ingredients	
easy		2 tbsp pine kernels, lightly toasted	GARNISH
		2 tbsp chopped fresh parsley	twists of lemon
serves 4		2 tbsp chopped fresh thyme	sprigs of fresh thyme
		1 garlic clove, chopped	
		1 tbsp grated lemon rind	fresh green and red salad leaves,
15–20 minutes		salt and pepper	to serve
		4 large, skinless chicken breasts	
		250 g/9 oz blue cheese, such as	
10–12 minutes		Stilton, crumbled	

Put the pine kernels into a food processor with the parsley, thyme, garlic and lemon rind. Season with salt and pepper.

Pound the chicken breasts lightly to flatten them. Spread them on one side with the pine kernel mixture, then top with the cheese. Roll them up from one short end to the other, so that the filling is enclosed. Wrap the rolls individually in aluminium foil, and seal well. Transfer into a steamer, or a colander placed over a pan of boiling water, cover tightly and steam for 10–12 minutes, or until cooked through.

Arrange the salad leaves on a large serving platter. Remove the chicken from the heat, discard the foil and cut the chicken rolls into slices. Arrange the slices over the salad leaves, garnish with twists of lemon and sprigs of thyme, and serve.

poached chicken
with brandy & cream

		ingredients	
very easy	1 tbsp butter	3 tbsp brandy
	1 garlic clove, chopped	salt and pepper
serves 4	2 onions, chopped	150 ml/5 fl oz single cream
	450 ml/16 fl oz chicken stock	
	1 tbsp chopped fresh tarragon	GARNISH
	4 large, skinless chicken breasts	sprigs of fresh flat-leaved parsley
15 minutes	1 large tsp cornflour	seedless white grapes, halved
	2 tbsp water	
17–20 minutes		freshly cooked tagliatelle, to serve

Melt the butter in a large saucepan over a low heat. Add the garlic and onions and cook, stirring, for 3 minutes. Add the stock and half of the tarragon and bring to the boil. Lower the heat, add the chicken breasts and cook for 10–12 minutes, or until cooked all the way through.

Lift out the chicken, cut into slices and keep warm. Strain the chicken stock and reserve. Discard the solids. In a separate large, heatproof bowl, mix the cornflour with 2 tablespoons of water, then gradually stir in the stock. Return to the saucepan and cook, stirring gently for 1 minute, then pour in the brandy. Season with salt and pepper and the remaining tarragon. Bring to the boil, lower the heat and cook, stirring, for 1 minute. Remove from the heat and stir in the cream.

Arrange the cooked pasta on a large serving platter. Arrange the chicken slices over the top and pour over the brandy sauce.Garnish with sprigs of parsley and halved white grapes and serve.

index